KABUKI

by Yasuji Toita
& Chiaki Yoshida

Translated
by Fred Dunbar

COLOR BOOKS

HOIKUSHA

K A B U K I

by Yasuji Toita & Chiaki Yoshida

Copyright © 1967

HOIKUSHA PUBLISHING CO., LTD.

20, 1-chome, Uchikyuhoji-machi, Higashi-ku, Osaka, 540 Japan

Fourth Edition, Sept. 1969

Printed in Japan

FOREWORD

Kabuki is the national classical theatre of Japan, noted for its color, beauty and the faithful representation of ancient customs and manners. A dancing priestess originated it in 1586. In 1629 on reasons of morality, women were forbidden to appear on any stage, young boys taking their parts, and from 1652 Kabuki was played only by adult males, gradually developing into the most perfect and elaborate theatre with its song, dance and skill.

Kabuki is originally so constructed that those who often go to see it can easily grasp the casting and the scene by just a glance at the color of the costumes and listening to the music played. For the first-timers, however, it might be difficult to understand what the scene signifies without any preparatory knowledge about Kabuki. There is, since olden times, an agreement between the stage and the audience, in other words, rules have to be followed without which we cannot fully appreciate the Kabuki play, it is like there are rules in the games of sports.

In this book I tried to introduce such rules in the world of Kabuki and also as many various aspects as possible within these limited pages.

Yasuji Toita

CONTENTS

Formal Curtain

In Kabuki the draw curtain is generally termed the "maku". Strips of three colors, black, reddish brown and green are joined together vertically. Each color represents a formal style and the three blended together

in the familiar Draw Curtain represents Kabuki.

The first thing which strikes the eye on entering the theatre is the Aisle Stage within the seats of the audience and the Formal Curtain. The sound of wooden clackers is soon heard and curtain time nears.

3

Backstage

Bustling activity is witnessed here just before curtain time. The expediter called "Kyogen Saku Sha" beats his clappers (left pics.) to notify all the start to draw curtain is approaching. Scene and property men make last minute checks seeking for any faults. The actor comes on stage and silently waits.

Page 5, Onoe Baiko in the play "Fuji Musume". The men in black are secne men, small property men and dress changers. The musicians are tuning their instruments.

4   Fuji Musume ▶

Curtain Time

The curtain opens. On stage the dance of the spirit of the Wisteria Flower represented by a young girl begins. It is done in a sweet and lovely background of large wisteria blossoms. The performance of a female, so well perceived in its intricacies, unfolds itself under the impersonation of Baiko. The role is the female part called "Onna Gata".

Fuji Musume

Make-up of the Female Impersonator.

In Kabuki the role of the female is played by males. The disguised actor is called Onna Gata. In Tokugawa days the Government prohibited females to appear on the stage. Inevitably, the Onna Gata was created by men who made this form of acting exclusive. It is their devoted hard efforts in acting this part that the art has been refined to an unexampled and unique status of today.

Bottom picture shows Naka-mura Utaemon cleaning his fingernails, a true sign of the Onna Gata's care for female neatness. On top·page, a light oil is used for base and the powder applied. In the process the eyebrows and lips are obliterated. The peony-shaped brush evens the powder. Lips are now rouged to shape and the eyelids painted. Note how the rested hand guides brush to draw lines in outer corners of eyes and also the way eyebrows are drawn with sumi-ink. Next, the hands and feet are powdered. The costume is worn and finally the hairdresser (toko-yama) places on the wig.

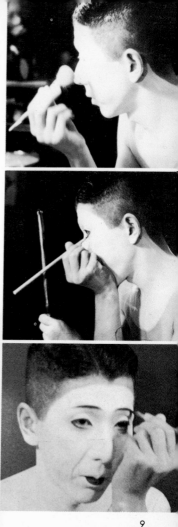

The Dance in Kabuki

A woman's beauty is manifested to the utmost in the dance, and "Musume Dojoji" is one of the masterpieces of Kabuki. Here we have Nakamura Utaemon in his forte.

A woman's vindictiveness changes her into a serpent to chase the man she loves. The legend of the man being burned together with the hanging bell of Dojoji Temple, was dramatized in Noh. Kabuki's adaption furthered it to where a new bell is hung. To this the spirit of the serpent appears in the guise of an itinerant entertainer (shira byoshi). Her dance develops gradually from the human into the realistic movements of a serpent.

Musume Dojoji

11

Rendition of "MUSUME DOJOJI"

What is mostly expected in the legend of "Musume Dojoji" is not the story, but the finesse displayed in its dances.

The "shira byoshi" describes by rhythmic movements the background of how she travelled to the temple. This is done along the aisle stage until the main stage is reached. An "eboshi" cap is then worn and the formal Noh dance for this is peformed, but it soon breaks into Kabuki. It then divides into various parts, each dance changing in mood with the costume changes done right on stage. Contained in these are the various technical skills or exercises of the "odori". They serve to highlight the Onna Gata's proficiency. Also used in each interlude are various small properties like, towels, drums and hats. The colors and sounds of these further set the dancer to advantage.

Dance with Tambourine   Dance with Hand Drum

Dance with Towel

Dance with Hats

Palm Movement Dance

Closing Scene of "MUSUME DOJOJI"

As the Shira byoshi reveals its true identity, a hero named Odate Samagoro appears on the aisle stage and subdues it. The finale comes when both stars and the assistants who form the body and tail of the serpent, come to a standstill, a pose. This tableau presentation is unique to colorful Kabuki. (Odate is represented by Onoe Baiko and Shira byoshi by Ichimura Uzaemon).

The SERI-DASHI Elevator.

Usually actors ascend on stage by lifts located in the side-aisles, but sometimes they rise from special traps cut on the main stage. These entries are usually for knights, ghosts and magicians. Frequently it is used when the vitality of a dance of the actor can be presented more effectively. Scenes are from the Salt Gatherer as Onoe Baiko arises from the aisle-stage elevator.

Shiokumi

Kanjin-cho

"KANJIN-CHO" Legend of the Subscription List.

The Kanjin-cho play makes use of Nagauta style singing, music accompaniment and dance acts. In substance it is extremely full of dramatic situations and in these instances, the Nagauta songs take the same part as Gidayu Kyogen of Gidayu singing which we will explain later.

The story is about a beaten warrior escaping with a few retainers disguised as soliciting priests. As they cross the barrier check-point of Ataka, their ruse is sensed by its keeper Togashi Saemon. Benkei, chief retainer of the hero Yoshitsune, by his quick thinking saves the party. The emotional and forceful scenes of the play makes it a favorite of the public, and is considered one of the masterpieces of Kabuki, a Juhachi-Ban.

Kneeling in the picture is Yoshitsune by Onoe Baiko, Benkei by Onoe Shoroku and Togashi by Ichikawa Danjuro.

Kenuki

JUHACHI-BAN—Favorite Kabuki Plays.

Actors from the famous families of Kabuki have traditional plays handed down to them. This repertoire is their
forte called the Juhachi-Ban.

Ichikawa Danjuro VII, reprentative of the famous Kabuki
family, made a pick of eighteen "kyogen" drama. Their
first ancestor originated the "Aragoto" or vigorous hero
plays. This characteristic style is a heroism portrayed by
grandiose and exaggerated ways in the use of make-up and
acting. Super-abundant strength is manifested in all its
phases. This stylised form has been brought to its highest
peak in Kabuki.

We see Ichikawa Danjuro in the mystery drama "Kenuki"
(hair pincers), staring at the exaggerated standing twe-
ezers. From this he deduces there is a magnet concealed

Zobiki

in the ceiling. "Zobiki" or elephant pulling, shows hero Kawarazaki Chojuro contesting for an elephant (dummy) with magician Nakamura Kanemon. Their ferocious strength eventually splits the elephant.

In "Ya no Ne" "Arrowhead" Ichimura Uzaemon as Soga no Goro is grinding his grotesque arrow on a gigantic sharpening stone.

Ya no Ne

"SUKEROKU"

Another popular Juhachi-Ban piece is the story of the gallant Sukeroku, his courtesan sweetheart Agemaki and the rich villain Ikyu. The plot is about the recovery of a stolen sword.

The setting is Yoshiwara, Edo City's foremost entertainment center, and very elaborately made. The gorgeous costumes and acting exude the culture of the merchant classes. It exceeds the other Aragoto plays in stylishness and specialises in amoirousness.

The picture is of Ichikawa Danjuro as Sukeroku going into his dance on the side aisle. The various beautiful poses taken truly stir the audience.

Sukeroku

23

The Love Scene.

The love scene is always a highpoint in Kabuki. Various pieces require appropriate acting, but audaciousness is common to all. The bold acting arises from the fact that the Onna Gata has to out-female any real female. Magnified actions are used to make the natural look more realistic.

Pictured top of page twenty-four is a scene from Nozaki Mura, a tale of a townsman's daughter and the lover apprentice of the house. Lower, Nao Zamurai relates the love of a courtesan and her client. Top of p. 25 is Nijushi Ko, a love story between a warrior's daughter and a young lord. Bottom is from Sukeroku.

Though the material of the plays are all different, the part of the woman is always forward and positive. In the movements of the dance, the pose is created to emote great beauty. These points are common to all acts of this kind.

Nao Zamurai

Nijushi Ko

Sukeroku ▶

Plays on Brothel Districts.

The brothel district appears frequently in Kabuki. It was the playground for the plain citizen. Only here could love be enjoyed in full without restrictions, during those strictly-controlled feudal days. As such, it offered the best in materials for the theater.

The tragedy, "Kago - Tsurube" is about fiendish peasant "Jiro-zaemon's" love for highest grade courtesan Yatsuhashi of Yoshi-wara. In the beginning scene he falls in love at first sight. Not seen in our picture he gazes fix-edly on Yatsuhashi as played by Nakamura Utaemon who is at-tired in the most formal dress of the courtesan. The trappings are simlply splendid.

Kago - Tsurube.

Scorned-Love Plays. AISO-ZUKASHI.

Situations of contempt are found in European love stories such as "Carmen". In Kabuki this circumstance is often found and usually in public scenes, thus making them to become more spiteful grudge causes.

"Chijimiya Shinsuke" is of this type (p. 28). The geisha Miyokichi is abandoned with despair and in her anger finds fault with the guest she likes. Usually in such stories, the girl really loves the man and though her heart may be true, she somehow manages to create a scene of contempt.

"Gosho Gorozo" is a good example (p. 29), the courtesan Satsuki is doing her best to raise money which her lover Gorozo needs. She however plays up to the villain Doemon, even though she has no feelings towards him, this disgraces her love for Gorozo.

Gosho Gorozo ▶

hijimiya Shinsuke

Ise Ondo

29

Scenes of Break-ups. ENGIRI.

In Scorned Love plays the break-up is the scene where the man becomes disgusted with the woman. A climax in the play, the acting is then extremely elegant. The woman endures the sorrows of her heart as she berates the man, whilst the man in anger speaks of his love-torn betrayal. The highest technique in the speaking of lines is now effected while in the background a special wind instrument, with gentle and plaintive sounds, mounts up the tension.

Here we give two scenes which give a pull on the heartstrings of the audience. Page 30 is from "Godai-Riki" as the geisha Koman, to appease the jealousy of the villain Sango-bei, breaks up with her lover "Gengo-bei". Page 31 is from Kago-Tsurube where Yatsuhashi the geisha disgusts her client.

Godai - Riki

Kago-Tsurube

Kago Tsurube

Omatsuri Sashichi

Onna Goroshi Abura Jigoku

32

The Kill Scene. KOROSHI-BA.

A man scorned usually kills the woman and this scene is often included in Kabuki. It is usual for a disgrace to develop into a killing, so much so that we can say it is a fixed plot. And to evoke more sympathy from the audience the hero in reverse is killed by his enemy.

Reflecting the feudal society then in existence, there are invariably many kill scenes in a play. On page 33 the bad man Toma in "Tenga-Chaya" kills the hero Iori. Page 32 top shows geisha Yatsuhashi being killed by crude Jiro-zaemon in "Kago-Tsurube".

Tenga-Chaya

Natsu Matsuri Naniwa no Kagami

Beautiful Death Scenes.

The best example of creating beauty in a brutal killing is seen in the play, "Natsu Matsuri Naniwa no Kagami". The principal, though a knave of a fisherman, kills for the sake of his house. His audacity lay in the slaying of his own greedy father in law, which was a serious social crime.

It is the latter's unbounded graspiness for money which finally makes hero Danshichi draw his sword. The kill is played up to its utmost refinement as we see Danshichi become undressed. The tattooed body and pretty loincloth display prominently as the actor gyrates into his Tachi-Mawari fight composed of many poses. This colorful and beautiful spectacle is increased with the backing of harmonious festival music.

Benten Kozo

The Fight.
TACHI-MAWARI.

The Tachi-Mawari fight not only appears in individual encounters but also in those against mobs. This latter form is similarly stylised to the extreme to give a good show. The music mingles with the beat of special clappers by which sounds the star is conducted to different pose making. The model for this type of fight can be found in the finale of "Benten-Kozo". The police, as they corner the hero on the rooftops, do somersaults and many other acrobatic movements which help to highlight the scene.

Benten-Kozo

The Spectacle of Large Scenery. AFURI-KAESHI.

Kabuki specialises in various spectacular scenes for the actor. One such display is in the use of large scenery changes. Its model is found in Benten-Kozo.

When the hero is finally cornered on the rooftops, he has no other means of escape except to commit hara-kiri. As he disembowels himself, the roof slowly folds upwards rising to give place to the gorgeous Cherry Gate where his companion Nippon Daemon is. Like the movies it has a wide screen effect with a perspective overlap.

Lives of Thieves. SHIRANAMI-MONO.

Another title for Benten-Kozo is "Shiranami Gonin Otoko" or Five Robbers. There are numerous plays in Kabuki which star the thief. Mokuami the late Tokugawa Era playwright wrote mainly on this theme. A reflection of the resentment on the conditions of the time. His best works are, "Izayoi Seishin", "Kochiyama", "Shima Chidori" and "Ikake Matsu".

The principals who appear are not really bad men, but are people to be sympathised with. Probably, defiance against authority appealed to the public when caused by undue circumstances. Their thievery is not highlighted, only their ordinary lives as they make their frequent appearances on the streets. It's the events which cause the transgressions that are pictured to evoke pathos.

"Ikake Matsu" is a play of a man turning robber becaus he is incited by a rich man's pleasure seeking. (top of p. 41.). "Shima Chidori" (bottom p. 41) relates the struggle between a man who has turned a new leaf and one who won't. "Kochiyama" (mid. pages 40-41) is a story of a thief impersonating a high ranking priest to force money out of a lord. "Izayoi Seishin" tells the story of a one-time priest and his mistress a former nun.

Izayoi Seishin

Ikake Matsu

Kochi Yama

Shima Chidori

Extortion Scenes.
YUSURI-BA.

In the Lives of Thieves Plays, the principal usually invents a pretext to exact money from someone. This extortion scene is called the Yusuri-Ba.

The incident seen in Benten-Kozo is well-known. He disguises himself as the daughter of a warrior family. With his accomplice Nango Rikimaru in samurai attire, they enter a clothing store. Kozo pretends to shop-lift for which he is slapped by a store attendant, whereupon the demands for redress begins. When it becomes evident he is a man, the situation changes, the kimono is bared at the shoulders to show tattooes and the blustering starts.

Benten Kozo

Clear Elocution

Most pleasant to the audience in the extortion scene are the musical lines uttered by the extorter accompanied by rhythmic postures which are fascinating. This form of bewitchery is laid on thick in these extortion scenes.

A good example is seen in "Genya Dana". The star Yosaburo is a rich man. He falls in love with another man's mistress, is found out and punished by having his body scarred all over. With no other resources he turns to thieving. Three years later he enters a house to extort the master and finds his former sweetheart Otomi there whom he thought dead. She again is a mistress and seems to be doing splendidly. Yosaburo grudges her for his present condition. The elocution used is so clear, fine and polished that it has always remained a favorite scene.

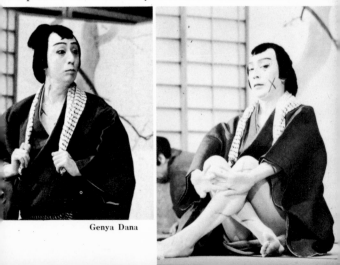

Genya Dana

Siranami Gonin Otoko

Famous Lines.
MEI-SERIFU.

The magic use of resonant speech to hold the audience is well prepared in Kabuki in various forms.

In the "Inase Gawa" act of Benten-Kozo, the five thieves appear before the law enforcers. Each declares himself singly. Since their personal characters are different, so are their narration with its accompanying music. The same with their proclamation, voice and manner. This kind of art effectively acts upon the audience exactly as the stage dictates.

Komochi Yamanba   Shibaraku

Art of Elocution. SHABERU GEI.

An essential element and very important to Kabuki is
the technique of elocution. The tone used by an actor
either makes or breaks his part of the play, no matter
how good the script may be.

The Onna Gata does not imitate the female voice, he
transfigures his male voice to give an illusion of resem-
blance which spell-bounds the audience.

In San Nin Kichiza is a robber disguised as a woman who
kills another woman by taking her money and pushing her
into the river. His impressions are chanted in a seven-
five rhythm. In contrast in Shibaraku, the principal goes
into a straight-out long narration.

San Nin Kichiza

Muscles and Nerve Line Make-up. KUMADORI.

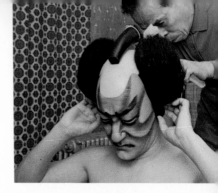

The style of Kumadori make-up was invented in connection with the Aragoto style of designating strength in super heroic proportions.

With the use of such colors as red, purple, black etc., the muscles and nerves are prominently exaggerated to enhance the impression desired. It also immediately tells the spectators the character depicted.

Generally speaking, red stands for loyalty and passion and purple for wantonness and viciousness.

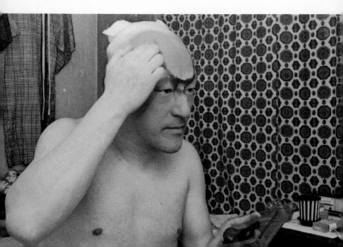

Contrasts. IN And YO.

The frank and the secret are often contrasted as a subject material. In the Sendai scene depicted under the floorboards of the house, the good hero Otokonosuke, with red facial lines, catches the villain transformed by

Sendaihagi

magic into a rat. Once caught the spell is broken, the
magician appears then on the aisle-stage in human form
wearing a mouse-grey dress and holds a scroll in his
mouth.

Standardised Hairdress and Costumes.

The costumes in Kabuki are not only gorgeous, they also indicate the social standing and character of the person wearing it. The hairdress also serves the same distinction. By the process of time, they have become so standardised that a spectator readily reads the character and situation at a glance.

In the preceding pages Nittsuki wears a hairdress which styles him as a traitor while Otokonosuke's hair shows him to be valiant and passionate. On this and the following page the shaved eyebrows and hairstyle represent a daughter of a warrior who is married. The way the sleeves of the dress are sewn signifies instantly she is a court lady. It is Masaoka in Sendaihagi.

Puppet Show Likeness.
GIDAYU KYOGEN.

Kabuki was founded at the same time as the puppet "Ningyo Joruri" show. It has taken in and absorbed many of its presentation forms.

Close to half of the acts performed in Kabuki are works from "Gidayu Kyogen" puppetry. The impressionistic art of the dolls were skillfully assimilated in live form and thus produced an unique style of beautiful presentation.

Sakaya

Kinkakuji

Kumagai Jin-ya

Its speciality lies foremost in good acting which co-ordinates with the gidayu singer and samisen player as one single unit, bottom p. 56. The actor is restricted to perform within certain stanzas of the song. The gidayu singer explains the time, place and movements of the actor and his mental state. In the "monogatari" form the past background is treated, page 57. A woman's sorrowing heart pleadingly sung is known as the "Kudoki", top page 56. These various forms combined make up what is called "Maru-hon Kabuki".

Chushingura

CHUSHINGURA. Forty-seven Loyal Retainers.

The best three plays taken from the puppet show are "Chushingura", "Yoshitsune Sen-Bon Zakura" and "Sugawara Denju Tenarai Kagami", co-authored by three writers.

Among them "Chushingura" or the story of the forty-seven loyal retainers is even known abroad, which was taken from an actual event of 1702. A lord is forced to draw his sword in court and for this show of temper is ordered to commit Hara-kiri. His loyal retainers then conspire to avenge his death. All eleven acts are even today staged and the showing is always very popular.

Three Deaths.

Kabuki very often shows the grave situation of a death scene to tighten the story together. It is however mostly of the Hara-kiri type, the method of the warrior and bespeaks of the age the play was made.

If we divide Chushingura into three parts, the death of Hangan in Act Four could be considered as the first. The death of Hayano in Act Six the second part and Kakogawa's death in Act Nine the third, each death making its point.

The death of Kakogawa (lower p. 61) is willingly induced by himself but through the instrument of another hand, that of Hangan and Kanpei and selfinflicted.

Kanpei, p. 61, dies as a masterless Ronin in a poor peasant's home while Hangan, p. 60, dies within a castle. The manners observed and the atmosphere they are conducted in are entirely different.

Chushingura

Chushingura ▶

◀ Chushingura

Yoshitsune Senbon Zakura

YOSHITSUNE SEN-BON ZAKURA.

This play though from the same writers as Chushingura is by far more romantic in its essentials. It centers around Yoshitsune the medieval warrior who defeated his strong enemy the Heike.

In " Daimotsu-Ura", the defeated enemy Taira no Tomomori, unable to seek revenge, ties himself to an anchor to meet his tragic end, page 62. We see the sad story of a young fox disguised as Yoshitsune's retainer in "Kawazura Yakata" page 63. It carries a hand-drum made from the pelt of its own parent to whom it was deeply attached.

63

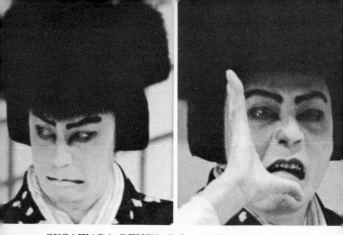

SUGAWARA DENJU. Tales of Sugawara Michizane.

This story dates back historically to the 10th century concerning two ministers of the court, Fujiwara and Sugawara. Sugawara has been falsely accused and exiled.

In the "Tera Koya" or village school episode, we see the deliberate and tragic placing of one's own son to be beheaded instead of Sugawara's. Done in so much secrecy the outcome is uncertain. Matsuo, former subject to Sugawara, now a retainer of Fujiwara has been sent to make sure the right head is being cut off. Matsuo has sent his son to the school incognito with the hope he will be sacrificed instead.

The suspense and agony of mind on the outcome is vividly shown on the facial expressions. Lower left p. 65, Matsuo is just handed the box containing the head. Lower right page 65, he opens the box and gazes` on the face of his son. Top pictures from left to right are; having handed over the container for the head, he listens intently for the beheading to be executed behind the screen panel. The instant the blade sings, the eyes fill up with tears. The container arrives but there is sorrow and uncertainty. Lastly, it's a shout of a job "Well Done".

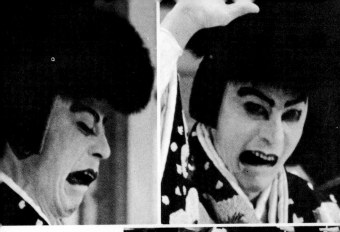

Sugawara Denju

65

Matsuo

Sugawara Denju

HIKIGOTO

In an earlier episode of Sugawara we have the three brothers, Sakura, Ume and Matsuomaru each contesting for possession of the palanquin of Fujiwara. Such pull-scenes in various forms appear in Kabuki as it was then a popular game among the people.

The facial lines, hairdress, costumes and swords are exaggerated in largeness to promote a scene of intense strength and vitality. Top page 67 is Ume and the bottom is Sakura and on page 66 is Matsu. In the bottom strip the palanquin is finally broken to pieces, Fujiwara stands in a costume denoting treacherousness and the three brothers are left absolutely spent in strength.

Sakuramaru

Kanjincho

Kawazura Yakata

Kagatobi

The Eyes.

During the act's progress there is a point on the stage where all seems to come to a stop while the figures form a tableau. This kind of special acting is called "Mie" and it is usually to point out the excited state of emotions that are being represented.

With the sounds of drums and other effective musical instruments, the eyes of the actors move into stares and glares. This serves like a close-up in a movie, so to be effective, the actor has to be very proficient in letting his eyes speak for his inner feelings instead of his mouth.

Top p. 68, in Kanjincho we see Benkei's eyes suppressing his feelings. Bottom right, an expression of surprise, left of happiness. Left p. 69 of anger and on right to sorrow.

Soga Taimen   Syunkan

The Princess

The princesses who appear on the stage usually have brocades sewn on a red background and so are called aka-hime.

There are three main plays which bring the Onna Gata actor into prominence which is aspired to as an honor to perform and are called San Hime.

These are Nijushiko upper left p. 70, the white background of the dress signifies the girl Yaegaki to be possessed by a spirit. In the play she steals a helmet for her lover. In Kamakura Sandai-Ki, lower left, princess Toki urged by her sweetheart attempts to kill her father. In Kinkakuji page 71, princess Yuki lets herself be captured by her lover's enemy in order to save his life.

They are all passionate princesses striving to survive for the sake of love.

Kamakura Sandai-Ki

Gion Sairei Sinko-Ki

Jitsugoto

◀Aragoto

The Casting. YAKUGARA.

Generally the male casts are termed "Tachi Yaku" and the female the Onna Gata. Strictly speaking, however, a virtuous and serious person is the Tachi Yaku, the bad man the Kataki Yaku, the handsome young man the Ni-Mai-Me, the comic the San-Mai-Me. These are again subdivided into age group, character, etc, each having its own distinction. The female Onna Gata too is similarly classified.

Various instances shown here are the Aragoto in top page 72 right and bottom, strong in body, character and all things. On the right is a Kuge Aku. Page 73 left, the comic Sanmaime and right the Wagoto who is a gentle and handsome youth.

Wagoto

Sanmaime

Handsome Youth.
WAGOTO.

The Wagoto story originated in Osaka. In "Kuruwa Bunsyo" we find a fine example of this kind. When Izaemon, the son of a rich family, becomes penniless he begins to doubt his sweetheart Yugiri. A courtesan, her anxiety in not wishing to cause him any displeasure makes her fall ill. This is how she expresses her deep love, while Izaemon in his jealousy makes a pathetic and silly caricature.

Kuruwa Bunsho

75

**Suicide Pacts.
SHINJU-MONO.**

Double suicides were dramatised from " Wagoto" plays about the love and death of a couple. In the strict feudal age, people could not marry outside their station, only way open to them being joined together, was death.

The youth usually had his nice looks but no money or position. The girls were closely watched and restricted and the courtesan was living in a society where money counted most.

Dramas made out of these materials greatly appealed to the masses. Page 76 top, the couple decide to bridge their lives together in the afterworld. Lower, the pair wearing dresses of the same family crest. Page 77, the penniless lover under the floorboards steals a glance at his sweetheart while the rich client waits above. An expressive picture on love is blind.

Sonezaki Shinju

Play of UMEKAWA CHUBEI.

Though not a suicide play, it follows a similar vein. Moneyless Chubei the hero is entrusted with a packet of money that is sealed. Wealthy Yaemon the other suitor not only broadcasts Chubei's poor condition but tries to buy the release of the courtesan Umekawa for his own pleasures. Thus goaded Chubei breaks the seal of entrusted money, knowing full well that this action leads to certain death.

Koihikyaku Yamato Orai

Sound and Property Effects.

The staging of Kabuki uses in full all kinds of effects. The sounds usually come from the enclosed area on the left called the choshi-beya or harmony room. The big drum turns out the natural elements like rain, wind, snow, even mountains, sea or river scenery.

Crude symbolics are used everywhere for visual effects. For instance to show night turning into day, the background curtain is dropped to reveal a brighter scene. In Narugami we see how lightning and rain is illustrated on bottom of page 80. A simpler style is the hanging of symbols for thunderbolts and rain or usually the big drum with the wearing of umbrellas or rainwear are sufficient. Small pieces of paper triangularly cut are dropped from the ceiling accompanied by the sound or drum music.

Snow   Lightning and Rain

◄ Cloud

Rain ►

The Moon

New Year Specialties.

The Japanese have always been susceptible to season changes, more so during Edo times. The repertoire for the New Year was fixed to the revenge play of the Soga Brothers. Within the act there is an act called the "taimen" or meeting face. It is an all-star cast who have made

Soga Kyodai

the theater group of that season, similar
in a way to the finale of a revue. The
scene has been refined and systematized
to such perfection to this day that it is a
mustsee spectacle.

Michi Yuki

Flower Viewing Plays. HANAMI TSUKI.

In the month of April the plays usually have a flowery background. In Edo days the women attendants working at the palace were allowed a vacation to visit their families or relatives. They flocked to the theater instead. These flowery scenes were tailored for them or the plays depicted courtlady life such as Kagami Yama top page 85, Sendaihagi or Saya Ate on bottom left page 85. Sukeroku and Michi Yuki on page 84 had their stages blooming full of cherry blossoms. Bottom right of page 85 shows a willow tree budding with new leaves.

Kagami Yama

Saya Ate

Kamiyui Shinza

Summary Plays.

For the summer program controversial plays were avoided because of the hot sultry weather. Simple and light themes referring to summer customs were preferred.

Bloody scenes were treated to chill to the marrow, for instance, in Ise Ondo, the hero slays over ten people who are all attired in light summery wear. The whiteness reminds of funeral clothes and when the blood spurts on the white, the shock is enough for shivers.

Ise Ondo

Yotsuya Kaidan

Weird Ghostly Tales.

Another program important to summer presentation were the weird ghost plays whcih frightened and thrilled with suspense. The audience were literally chilled to their bones. Yotsuya Kaidan is a representative of this form. It is the story of Iemon who is instrumental in the poisoning of his wife and later killing her together with a servant. The ghosts then appear and haunt him to his death.

Kumagaya Jinya

Kiitsu Hogan

Shibaraku

Formal Introduction. KAO-MISE.

Yearly contracts made by the actors are renewed each November. New stars who are to make their debut with the group are also introduced to the public at the same time. This occasion appears during December and is incorporated in the play Shibaraku which was specially written for such a purpose.

91

Audience and Stage.

Kabuki has a special close connection with the spectator. There is the Hanamichi running among the audience seats and other forms which help to draw the spectator into the play itself.

In Banzui Chobei top page 93, the actor walks down the ordinary aisle for an entrance. Sometimes two aisle stages are used for acting as in Nozaki Mura page 92. The usual one represents the river and the extra one the embankment. In Musume Dojoji page 93, towels are thrown to the audience as presents while the dance is performed.

Nozaki Mura

Banzui Chobei ►

Musume
Dojoji

Two Aisle Stages.

The fullest effect of the two side stages are made in Yoshino Gawa. The audience is the middle of the river itself and the two stages the banks. As the spectator looks from one side to the other he is soon engrossed deeply enough to be drawn into the act.

Imoseyama

Exit by Aisle Stage.

Shibaraku

The performance of an exit from the stage is as important as the entry. When the final curtain is drawn, the actor who is left on the aisle stage retires with flourishing arms and legs amid shouts of encouragement.

Billboard (kabukiza)

THE THEATRE

A palpitation of excitement is created even before entering into the Kabuki Theatre itself. Such a feeling was more deeply evidenced during the Tokugawa days, when the theatre had a tower-like scaffold in the front. This was draped with banner standards which were dyed with the crests of the group then in performance. Such a turret was the symbol of the authority to conduct a theatre. They certainly gave a definite impression of the stronghold where the actors were to sway and command.

Such standards fluttered in the breeze up until the great earthquake of 1936, they were the presents from avid fans to their favorite stars. The practice of giving presents by the rich and poor to show esteem to a favorite actor is followed today although the former standards have changed into various different forms. They bear inscriptions such as, "Ichikawa Danjuro— EXCLUSIVE," which means to convey that the star is non-approachable in his Art.

During the Spring Season we find large casks of the rice-brew "sake" lined and piled outside the theatre. Presented to the theatre they bring famous brand names to the public eye and at the same time serve as ornaments. At the Minami-za in Kyoto during its December program, large rectangular boards termed "beckoning" have the names of actors of the new coming season inscribed on them. These are also aptly called boosters, for they come from the boosters themselves who are anxious and impatient to see the coming show.

Up to forty years ago there were tea-houses facing the theatre. Whenever the play Sukeroku was performed all the tea-houses were decorated to represent the Yoshi-wara district to conform with the inside of the theatre.

In these days every theatre is of modern structure and no longer holds such exhilarating characteristics. In spite of this, today's theatre-goer still experiences a thrill in his heart as he enters, is led through corridors past the doors and brought to his seat.

When Kabuki is performed on a stage the Formal Curtain comprising three colors is used. The reddish brown, green and black represent the three theatrical companies from Edo times, the Nakamura, the Ichimura and the Morita. Formerly, each company used its own colors but today they all use the three combined. This blend immediately strikes the eye as Kabuki.

As the spectator seats himself, he hears coming from behind the curtain, cries of heave-ho and hammerings as property men fix their scene scaffolding. When curtain time approaches, the expediter starts clacking his wooden clappers in a special two-beat. It is the cue for the costumed actors to get set on their mark as if ready for a great contest. These sounds are found very pleasing by the audience.

I definitely remember when I was a child that as soon as the curtain was to be drawn, my expectancy of the mysteries about to unfold and I always wished they'd hurry with the exposure. I would get more ex-cited during summertime for the side doors were left open and the air would billow the curtain. Then I managed to catch a few flashes of the happenings behind.

In today's theatre we find many other curtains besides the simple formal curtain, such as congratulatory curtains which are presented to an actor upon his succession to a house name. They are the gorgeously brocaded ones which are drawn successively during intermission time. We find five of them in the Kabuki Za.

It is however necessary that whenever there is a Kabuki Classic, the formal curtain by itself is drawn. This is because there should be no deterrent or impediment to the manner of opening or closing such curtains, for they are dictated by the beats of the wooden clappers which enhance the scene and also invigorate the exit of an actor who is left on the side stage after the curtain closes.

One is certain to find that there are many unique specialties in the art of Kabuki. From the first view of the formal curtain the stage starts and continues to unfold surprises which are always beyond expectations. Some may appear to be very rude or to be very rational. Whatever they may seem, discoveries will be made of inimitable visual and aural presentation methods which are peculiar to Kabuki techniques. Such disclosures are certainly to be looked forward to for appreciation.

MAIN THEATRES WHERE
KABUKI IS PERFORMED

TOKYO

    Kabuki Za   Shinbashi Embujo

    Meiji Za   Tokyo Takarazuka Hall

    Geijitsu Za   Nissei Theatre

    Toyoko Hall   Yomiuri Hall

    National Theatre   Teikoku Theatre

OSAKA

    Shin Kabuki Za   Asahi Za

    Naka Za   Umeda Koma Theatre

    Osaka Sankei Kaikan Mainichi Hall

KYOTO

    Kyoto Minamiza

NAGOYA

    Nagoya Misono Za   Meitetsu Hall

THE AISLE STAGE

The stage which is situated along the sides of the audience seats that runs at right angles to the main stage is called the "HANA MICHI" or flower path.

This side stage, 1.8 metres wide, is used for a special entry and exit of actors to and from the main stage. Its opening is on the furthest part from the main stage and has a black cloth curtain bearing a white insignia of the performing group.

In certain plays this entrance curtain is replaced by others. When adapted Noh plays are performed, a rising curtain made up of five colors sewn vertically in strips is used. In the Chushingura play it is changed to a cedar door.

The ordinary curtain is pushed from right to left as the actor enters, the jingle of curtain rings as they slide along the rod sounds a moment of expectancy to the audience. In some plays where tension is to be created no sound is made heard. This is to catch the audience unawares so that the actor seems to have appeared from nowhere.

Although the opening of this curtain may be a slight thing, many an actor's performance for the day has been spoiled if it is not successfully conducted. The very moods of an actor has to be reflected in the sound of the sliding rings. This slight act is a performance in itself.

It is usual for the footlights on the aisle stage to be turned on so as to signal the approach of an actor to the stage. In such instances like when the curtain is opened noiselessly, no such warning lights are lit.

Actor Uzaemon XVth was reluctant to have the side lights on full brightness as he wished to efface his elderliness. Very bright lights bring an effect of Spring, but lighting can be manipulated to create a performance of art on its own merit.

In stylised-pose plays such as Shiranami Go Nin Otoko, the performance stakes itself on the beauty of appearances of the entire assembly of the stage, even though each star is individually highlighted. The whole stage seems so naturally lighted yet each of the five stars exudes with an individual luxurious aura which does not clash. Each individual's entrance is accompanied by music specially written to agree with the star. This ingenious ringing accompaniment fills the heart deep with buoyancy. It is only in this play where we see an assistant handling the umbrella written with the large characters of the variant hero. Out of the entrance it is forcefully thrust open and handed over to the actor with a shout of encouragement. This makes a very florid entrance indeed.

Behind the curtain where the actor waits for his cue, is a full sized mirror such as are found in the Noh stage. In this alcove quick and instant dress changes are made for certain plays. In comedy scenes it is usual for the actors to crack jokes with each other in low tones while waiting for their entrances. This jovial atmosphere is then transferred onto the stage. But when the part requires seriousness the actor is found with his head down in serious contemplation while the rest of the actors are quiet and apart.

In the play "Kagami Yama," the elder of the house

is scolded by the lady-in-waiting and exits the aisle stage with head down. Some time elapses before he makes his re-entry in the same dejected manner. When actor Onoe played this part, it is said that he maintained the same attitude and stance all the while he was backstage. The other actors would not talk to him as they were afraid to spoil his mental attitude for the coming scene.

The aisle stage in Kabuki has the same function as that of Noh. The only difference is that the former passes through the audience while the latter slants from the stage slightly towards the back.

The hana-michi is where the actor is able to put out his hand and grasp that of the spectator. The meaning of this is significant for Kabuki strives at a closer attachment with the audience. The fan is elated because he can get a real close-up view of his favorite actor. When the lights flare up on the side aisle with the appearance of their expected star, shouts of "We've been waiting, MATTE MASHITA," "So and so YA" which is the family name of the actor.

In the play Dojoji, the shira byoshi dancer singer sits on the side aisle and throws small balls of paper to the fans who eagerly struggle for such keepsakes. This has now developed into the towel throwing done while in the dance act.

The side aisle is an extension of the stage and one may be justified in considering it as a road only a few paces away from the stage building. As, when, Benten Kozo in the play Shiranami asks for the dry-goods merchant's house, it signifies a distance which is little further. Nevertheless the aisle stage can also be considered at times to be as something separate, such as when Sukeroku goes there and personally introduces himself to the audience with singing and dancing. While this is going on, the main stage has come to a standstill until it is joined by Sukeroku.

The length of the aisle stage is about 18 metres and the seven-tenth way mark was considered to be the proper spot for an actor to make his introductory performance. Nowadays it is much nearer to the stage probably made necessary to give the viewers in the third-story seats and standing-room only a chance to see.

As stated before it was at this seven-tenth spot where the actor went into his specially fixed poses. And it is there where the trap-door which rises and falls is located. This entrance and exit pit is used mainly for other than human characters such as ghosts and magicians.

In the play Nittsuki Danjo, the rat-disguised magician is subdued by the hero on the main stage. When the rat is cut in two by an iron fan it disappears from sight by the aisle trap-door. A column of smoke then arises and from its midst we see the re-appearance of the magician in his mouse-grey costume.

In connection with this play it may be mentioned that whoever plays the part of the hero Nittsuki, always wears on his costume the family crest of the great actor Koshiro. And never forgotten in make-up is the addition of his distinctive mole located at the tip of the actor's eyebrows. This pays homage to that great actor and illustrates how proud Kabuki is about tradition.

We now see that the side aisle is where the stage

performers display their ostentatious histrionics. In Do-joji, the group that makes up the serpent's body comes to this area to perform an intricate dance in tune to the jangling beat made from special bells. In Seki no To, both Sekibei and Sumizome who are talking about the pleasure district step on purpose to the side aisle to show off their dramatic powers. During a kill-scene on the main stage we see the actor brandishing his sword. He then runs in step to clapper beats to the boundary between aisle and stage. His looking around to see whether there are any witnesses to his slaughter is another of those accepted rules contained in Kabuki. In a dance act, the actor using the side entrance always dances a passage to the song being sung before gaining the main stage. In the play Shibaraku, the star narrates here a summary of his role in some length. We can even say that the side aisle is used as a place to make a prologue before entering into the main theme.

In such cases when the main curtain closes and leaves the actor on the side aisle, he sometimes makes his exit with peculiar steps and bounds which is another method of magnifying mimic art for presentation to the audience.

Although the usual side aisle is to the left of the audience, there are certain plays which require another right aisle to double the effect. In this case the two sides can then be the banks of a river with the audience the river itself. They follow the play by swinging their sights to both embankments. There are some instances when the actors descend from the stage and ply between the seats of the audience and make their departure through the side-stage entrance. This method gives the property men time to set the stage for the next act. Such forms of theater is much appreciated by the fans which gives them an opportunity of close proximity with their favorite stars.

The use of two side stages is much desired, but we can see that the fixing of the temporary one makes for removal of some spectator seats. This clashes with the theatre management's expediency of selling as many seats as possible, which is a pity.

The Aisle Stage

THE PERFORMANCE

During its long history Kabuki has naturally advanced and arranged each of its traditional plays. The basic aim of Kabuki is to exhibit a person's individuality by such smooth movements which results in a presentation of forms which are then beautiful in aspect.

The acting formula, or kata, is that certain style which was specialised by a former leading actor. This is handed down from generation to generation by members of its house or family, whether it be from father to son or from teacher to apprentice.

Not only does this apply to movements alone, it also comprises theatrical elocution, make-up, dressing, the use and handling of large scenery and small property, even extending to script arrangements and accompanying music. It truly covers a very wide field.

Each traditional formula is not only treasured highly but each and every phase is at the same time bound by a hard and fast rule of making it appear realistically beautiful whenever presented. Take for instance the role of Kanpei in Chushingura who is supposed to be the most handsome of all in the play. He is handicapped when he turns into the role of a hunter, but his portrayal is not country bumpkin-ish at all, it has the air of a citified dandy. In this act there is the scene where he fatally shoots Sadakuro mistaking him for a bear. Kanpei approaches the body in utter darkness, however he is holding a lit match wick for his gun. From the beginning this tiny fire is virtually unseen by the audience, but it is there all the same.

When the scene turns dark this is put out, again unnoticed by the spectators, in a special stage prop composed of a bamboo cutting filled with water and which is hung on a nearby pine tree. All this can be said to be unnecessary, but it is a paying of close attention to the smallest of details which helps to promote the mood of the actor. A little later we see Kanpei lifting the purse tied to a string which is hung around Sadakuro's neck. Now, this cord was first seen to be rather short and here it has been substituted for one much longer. This is done because the scene has to show how the cord catches on the hunting blade and is cut in the process.

The lengthy string gives a close-up illustration to the audience, it also dispenses with Kanpei having to take a posture which would have a clumsy appearance. The essence of presenting a scene in its best form is evident here.

These tricks of the trade in showing everything to the best of advantage have been handed down from mouth to mouth and form the rules which abide in Kabuki.

In a Kabuki performance it has always been the leader of the troupe who dispensed with the roles for the play and such is understandable under the starring system. There have however been quite a few leaders who have created roles to suit themselves.

In any play there are always scenes where the supporting cast besides the stars have a chance to display their theatricals, but these scenes have from time to time been pared down to fatten the roles of the stars.

We now see in the play "Kuruma Hiki" of the three

brothers that two of them are dressed in red while one is dressed in white. Of course the contrasting role is reserved for the leader to display his own special brand of acting to an advantage.

Such picking of roles to suit one's purpose have swerved away from the contents of the original play. Instead of arranging parts between the stars themselves, it is about time a reversion was made back to the former script and plays conducted with a faithfully renditioning as originally planned.

Actors who will go according to script are now needed and desired and furthermore they should pay more attention and consideration to picture-like effects and the music itself has to be restudied carefully. It is also hoped that actors convey their voices more better so that they can be clearly heard and understood.

It is also to be noted that some dances, songs and text have retained the not-so-good mannerisms and habits of past masters and they are being repeated today as traditional. Such peculiarities have cluttered the body of Kabuki and these are among the number of defects which should again be weeded out.

Kisen

THE ACTING

Kabuki acting does not, like the modern drama, project man's doings by realistic mannerisms in voice and movement, though in the "Sewa Kyogen" we find some of it to make the audience shout "komakai," fine to the last detail. These are limited.

The actor always strives to make his voice and postures as beautiful as possible and in no instance should this be forgotten.

Classic drama was begot from Kabuki. Even in the 300 odd year history of "Aragoto" brave ruffian plays, and in the "Maru Hon Mono" written for puppets, the presentations are far separated from realism.

Though the mannerism and script are bound in a world of imagery, the actor has to draw the audience into this illusion. He is then ever obliged to cultivate his onstage voice and to constantly practice his basic stage movements.

The "Aragoto" was originated by Ichikawa Danjuro I and refined by the son in the second generation. It was unique acting which definitely reflected the character of the Edo people of those days.

The star was a superlative hero. He outstretched his arms and legs as much as possible and exerted to hold himself fast with an extreme effort. He represented an attitude of peerlessness in the world. The big toe of the thrusted foot in front had to point straight heavenwards. Irrespective of all this, the handed down rule says he must perform like a mischievous five or six year old, boy, that is to be naive.

His voice had to be high and clear and contain some hint of a provincial accent.

The tableau "mie" stance of the aragoto is to be as stationary as a statue. A frozen figure, the right hand is outstretched, the left wrist twistingly set under the chin and the right foot launched out. Combined they represent a forceful form. In rhythmic succession other forms are made to fascinate the audience with each formation taking a realistic meaning.

The substance of some acts are nonsense and have been contrived just for the stance.

Several actors crisscross right and left in the silent "danmari" scene to present their mie. Towards the closing scene of some drama while the wooden clappers are beating away for the finale a tableau is made by a trio. The star in the middle may then mount a red blanketed bench and present his last big stance. At times his personal prompter assists from behind to arrange the costume in such a way as to magnify his appearance while the actor struggles to enlarge his facial expressions. The highest accolade an actor can receive is that he has impressed a larger stature of himself on the audience.

The general rule is that the stance should be conducted facing the audience squarely. During a conversation the co-star also strives to face the audience as much as possible without turning his back on the star. In the mie the neck is also turned around in rhythmic movements. The female impersonators or youngsters do not go into a stance but always arrange themselves in pretty forms.

Kabuki being an entertainment for the masses has

love scenes. What typifies torrid sex is impressively conveyed to the audience by the actors by merely the placing of shoulders on knees, patting each other's cheeks or just holding hands and gazing. The way it was done sufficed to satisfy the audience.

There are different fixed forms for laughter and tears which are really affective. The stringed samisen music plays its part and at times the chanter offstage is joined in by the actor to form a duet. The dialogue is frequently attuned to movements and expressions. An episode is clearly typified within a certain framework of musical sounds or uttered exclamations, like hoy, ya, sa or da. Formality in Noh play decrees that in crying, the hand is to be raised to the mask. We find the same set frameworks in Kabuki, as say, within a tense uneasy situation the two actors are bound to turn clockwise while staring at each other.

Tsukemawashi

ONNA GATA
THE FEMALE IMPERSONATOR

What probably catches the eye of the first timer to Kabuki is the man dressed in woman's garb. It is the "Onna Gata."

Originally Kabuki was formed by women but for moral reasons they were banned by the Tokugawa authorities during the 17th century. Since then males have taken the female parts thus setting a long tradition.

Roles in Kabuki are separated into the good man called "Tate," the enemy called "Kataki," woman "Onna," oldster "Rojin," children "kodomo" and funny man "Doke."

In the beginning each role was specialised but later a few achieved to manage to take on every part. And so depending on the actor's individual versatility some roles became his personal forte and the same holds true today.

There are some female impersonators who hail from specialised and established theater families such as Utaemon and Fukusuke of the Narikoma-ya.

The gentle type of male is naturally suited for this role, nevertheless from the start he is physically handicapped by his hard and harsh body lines to produce a true personification. To overcome this unnaturalness the onna gata has to make great efforts to emphasize such elegance which is found missing in the real female. A style of amorousness which is lacking is then displayed on the stage.

In Noh play this amorousness is classified as "hana"

flower and this is the aesthetic performance of a Kabuki play where everything is contrived for as beautiful a presentation as possible. The onna gata must succeed to make a young girl's role especially charming.

The roles of town girl, country girls of high born families are called the "aka-hime." These roles with that of the courtesan are so conducted to appear unsophisticated, it is an established rule.

During the first hundred years when the males took up Kabuki, the dances were left under the care and management of the female impersonator. The role of the weaker sex compelled them to act with their eyes cast downwards, even when the opportunity arose for their scenes to be highlighted. Their location had to be at least a metre behind the male.

Therefore when it came to the dance which was left in their hands, they went all out without stops. The audience were treated to all the beautiful arts which could possibly be found in dance form. In the "Dojoji" dance not only are the costumes constantly changed within the act but each time it is followed with different step forms. It is believed that in this dance every variable passion and pose that a young girl has, is displayed. This dance is performed by women outside but it cannot be denied that only the onna gata can give it full justice.

In Tokugawa days the brothel quarters were the salons of entertainment. The popular songs and dances were those that relieved the spirits of the women living there. Buddhists in those days also taught that women in general were bound for sufferings in the next world to come. That was their fate. Kabuki in its dances took in these distresses and sorrows known only to the women. They were captivatingly done on the stage by the female impersonator.

In elopement plays and here and there in puppet derived plays there are seduction scenes where the woman delicately acts to outline her mental process. Usually the man is there listening in annoyment at such feelings. Most of the conversation is chanted in song by the master singer on the sidestage or backstage and the music in this case is refined for good listening. It is a part where the female impersonator has his chance to display and glorify his acting talents to advantage.

By feudal concept the woman in Kabuki acts gentle and sincere to her man. However in the complicated pieces, the girl for some reason not in her heart has to alienate the man's love purposely. The words of severance are played to the accompaniment of a special three-stringed instrument whose timbre symbolises pathetically the sobs in the girl's heart.

When the man does not learn the real truth as to motives for the separation, he in anger usually turns a blade on her. The scene then evolves into a murder. Yet such a brutal scene is performed beautifully. The ou le move consonant to the chanting by separating and entangling. The audience soon finds itself enticed into the delirium raised by Kabuki.

STYLE OF DRESSING

Another of the delightful and pleasant sights to see in Kabuki is how the actors dress. The dress, like the scenery, can also be termed "joshiki" standard, for what an actor is to wear in a certain role has already been fixed within a framework.

The rule for a lady of noble birth is a red brocaded long-sleeved kimono with a wig decorated by a flowery hairpin. So when one appears likewise we may assume she is a court lady, noblewoman or of other noble birth. Termed the "aka-hime" red lady, she rarely puts her fingers outside her sleeves. The right sleeve is placed on the breast and the left is open. She is readily recognised for what she is by the audience.

The quick-witted serving man of a great household wears a colored "jusu" dress. Gorgeously adapted from the liveryman's half-coat, it is so designed to enhance the handsomeness of the actor's figure.

Textiles used for the hero's outer and under wears are excellent. In some instances they are decorated by large family crests of the actors. When they appear in a group one marvels in astonishment at the keen perception the originators had for color schemes.

The dresses themselves lend a great effect on the movements of the actors. Like the lining of a dress, a person's psychological moment is expressed and described with each change of dress. Unique to Kabuki are the methods of quick changing of dresses onstage, for immediately another majestic aspect stands revealed before the eyes. These changes happen more than once on the set, there being five in the Sukeroku play.

The onna-gata playing the super courtesan is heavily draped with dresses and belts which would weigh down any ordinary person. The dignity of upholding their role seems to keep them up.

Dress does not mean costumes alone. Wigs are also used to define station in life, circumstance and character. Minute changes can be seen of the wig since there are many for various occasions. Sometimes a hair accessory helps to give it another meaning. So called lion manes are used for the powerfully brave. The hairs on these bristle up straight as on an angry wolf's back. The art of make-up in putting colored streaks on faces also defines an actor's inward emotions.

An admirable tradition in Kakuki is that a quick rough estimate can be established of the character depicted just by looking at the costume, wig or make-up.

EQUIPMENT INSTALLATIONS

The stage installations go by the name of large scenery "O-Dogu" and the rest by small props "Ko-Dogu."

Recently these have become extravagant, but strictly speaking Kabuki can get by with simple property since in some cases it is better to have them in a rough condition. A solitary pine tree in front of a drop curtain may suffice, or it might be balanced by a sheaf of rice and a reed mat fence. Abbreviation fits this form of theatre.

Ever since the early days when a scenario called for a palace mansion, shrine or the old homestead, they have all been the same with a few slight changes for scenes of different plays. The main street in the Yoshiwara gay quarters is always represented by tea-houses painted out of measurement on the right and left side of the backdrop while a grove of cherry trees appear in the center. Being so standardised one readily knows what the background is, just by the mention of mansion or old homestead.

The pillars of mansions always appear in black lacquer. Flower designs on the sliding and lintel panels seem like nothing, but they do brighten up the stage.

Only a part of a shrine gate or part of its moat is enough to signify its precincts. A short, parted, light yellow curtain hangs over the door of a homestead. Another special feature in Kabuki are the ostentatious movements made upon entry and exit through curtains.

Sliding screen door panels and windows are used for

hut, house or room constructions. An accent to the flow of the play is given when the principals open and shut them as occasion demands. The wooden sliding door once it has served its purpose may be immediately removed by the black-clad prompter to allow unobstructed views to the spectators, or only just to enhance the scene. It is unnatural but practical.

The removal of a series of screen doors in a room gives a newer aspect to the play with a creation of perspective views. In such cases, it signals that a final highlight to the act is about to commence.

Since the side-aisle exists in Kabuki, the front entrance to a dwelling is always located three steps away from this on the main stage. So fixed is this that the actor never fails to find it at all difficult to time and perform his movements.

To define a patch of ground, an earth colored cloth is spread. The actor who drops anything in this area instinctively wipes it free of dirt. Other coverings in use are the water and snow sheets called wave and snow cloths. The wave cloth is used to describe both river and sea scenes.

An ingenious device has been resorted to when a horse rider is supposed to ride far out into the sea. The full-sized man and horse dwindle into the distance as a child actor riding a toy horse replaces him. It is very naive but gives the imagery of perspective.

The attendant prompter in water and snow scenes blends himself with the background by using appropriate covering. His duties are to minister to the actor he is assigned to, by handing such props as are needed, re-arranging of dress and make-up, or placing a stool for him to sit on. The latter function is not as a seat but as a form of stabilisation in making the actor seem larger than usual.

A standard rule in Kabuki is that some things should remain unnoticed even when seen. When a black drop is used it is assumed that events are occuring in utter darkness as the actors act accordingly. This black curtain is at times dropped to describe the break of dawn.

If necessary a moon is spotlighted which at times appears and disappears to indicate light and then darkness. A sudden appearance of the moon equals the evening bell which announces. Such unnatural methods are found very natural within Kabuki.

Another natural feature to this theatre is the light-yellow drape curtain which is let fall at opportune moments. On occasions action continues in front of this, otherwise when no activity is seen the audience expects to be presented with a brilliant and dazzling display already being prepared behind it.

Trap-lifts are ingeniously made use of, for spectacular scenes bringing luxurious flowery settings onto the stage, while a special music is being played. It is breathtaking and always makes the hearts of the audience flutter.

The revolving stage is supposed to turn in a liberal flow with stops, shakes and spurts, and so should the trap-lift. But, alas, all goes too smooth today for electricity is used instead of man power.

The equipment ranging from the pretentious to the unpretentious all are constituted of simple factors and it is this which outlines the spirit of Kabuki.

SMALL PROPERTY

Props which are managed by the actors, those that are already placed on the stage or those that are handed to them, are in general termed small property "Ko-dogu." Viewed on stage are items of daily use, or those rarely seen, such as are stored up by anti-quarians or are in museums.

Long and short swords which were worn as custom decreed either by merchants or warriors are in evidence. The manner in which they are swingly raised or lowered is a pretty sight. The hero when cornered by a group flashes his sword in simple or complicated motions. The technique is by far from that of the real warriors and it is doubtful whether a person could be killed in such a fashion, anyway, these movements in dance form are certainly spectacular and nice to see. The blood on the blade may often be wiped off by another person. The extreme is when a person wears three swords. The sword as a prop is most often in evidence to the spectators.

It must be remembered that the ultimate factor in Kabuki is stylised beauty and so all the props are carefully planned to be handled in such a manner.

The kerchief of multiple purposes comes in a variety of colors and are distinctive to regulated roles. If the head, ears and cheeks are covered the purpose is to hide one's identity. When the female impersonator drapes it over her wig with one end clamped in the mouth, the face is partially obscured, making an effect which is retreating yet coquettish.

The manner in which a tobacco pipe is handled or held also gives clues to the circumstances the actor is in, for Kabuki also concerns itself with many minute details. By carefully watching a love disavowal scene, the courtesan can be seen to thrust, lay down or handle her pipe during the dialogue. They help to point out instant by instant her mental process.

The umbrella is often employed. The Japanese umbrella has an elegant appearance and so is used irrespective of rain. It is often brought into play in the dances and in the picture-like stance act.

Another item often appearing is the folded letter.

The horse

A letter from a courtesan can always be recognised from its red lines.

Amazing to the uninitiated is how a small battle-ax grows to double its size in the next act even though it purports to be the same one. Or, a warrior is supposed to be carrying his helmet wrapped on his back, which he actually does not. When the time comes for him to put it on, it is handed to him by the prompter. To enter and exit the stage with a bulky pack on the back of course does not look pleasant and so is avoided.

Also strange to see are the animals, the horse is played by two men for the fore and hind legs. The dog has a mask for its face with the body of a man. Mice and butterflies are attached on wire springs and manipulated by the prompters.

The cherry tree fixed on the stage is under the care of the large property men whilst a broken twig held by the actor is under the custody of small property men. It is therefore safe to assume that whatever the actor manipulates is small property.

MUSIC

Kabuki is a combination of different arts containing many essential elements. Since its inception to the present day, much has been digested in its great maw to become its blood and bones.

Music too, like the performance and all its pertinent parts, has for 300 years been created by composers whose names are mostly unknown. The music has been so arranged, planned and devised mainly to help the actor and it is still so done today.

Formerly the bandstand was located near the side-aisle stage which was so frequently in use for acting that the stand has now moved to the opposite end. Here the musicians who are exclusively attached to the theater play from peculiar annotated scores. This chamber has a narrow striped window and a black lacquered bamboo blind separates the musicians from the audience. To the professionals it is known as the black room while officially it is called the lower seat "geza."

The lower seat music can be divided roughly into three categories, the three-stringed banjo samisen, the samisen with vocal accompaniment and the percussion and wind instruments. The compositions and sounds that are played here are exclusive for Kabuki so it is impossible for an outside score to be played here.

The big drum is so attuned to distinctly sound different for various functions, such as, the first act opening, entry of troupe master and way on up to the finale. A wide application of the drumsticks results in such phenomena as mountains, rivers, seas, rain, snow, thunder or the appearance of ghosts and monsters.

The opening of a sea scene is made by wave sounds interspersed with a beach song. Besides this there is another sound for wave crests. In the snow scene a snow song follows it while a quietly struck bell is being sounded. When one becomes used to these sounds a picture of sea or snow comes easy to the mind.

In a ghost scene the big drum softly follows its motions and emphasises them. For this instance, a accepted rule is for the drum to be accompanied l a plaintive flute, while a fiery alcohol swab of cloth made to float in the air.

A small drum is employed to reproduce an ech . Combined with the big drum it activates the fight scene. The flute is used during hara-kiri and wh the woman goes into the disavowal of her man a fidd plaints. The hanging bell alerts the audience that a important part of the play is about to commence. Th biwa-lute preludes a mansion scene and a temple signified by Zen chants.

All these pre-ordained sounds follow the fixed ru of acting, and no subsitute has yet been found bett to take its place.

In such silent actions as hair-dressing, letter-writing or a couple making love, the geza sings a special song which follows the action.

The actor's art is either killed or aided accordin to the style each sound is produced or tuned. The have to be suited individually and intense experiment is necessary to discover them. Hard work dictates th right-sized drumstick beat, or when to play the samisen, whether before or after a dialogue or during a certain break.

It is very rare for a geza musician to give a show on the outside. The essential character of Kabuki music contrasts with other music in the use of instruments, songs, the timing of dances or in the impressions they are supposed to create.

To have a deeper appreciation of Kabuki is to begin to like its sounds.

HOIKUSHA COLOR BOOKS

—JAPANESE EDITIONS—

COLORED ILLUSTRATIONS FOR NATURALISTS

Text in Japanese, with index in Latin or English.

First Issues (Book Size 6" x 8")

1. BUTTERFLIES of JAPAN $10.00
2. INSECTS of JAPAN vol.1 $10.50
3. INSECTS of JAPAN vol.2 $ 9.50
4. SHELLS of JAPAN vol.1 $10.50
5. FISHES of JAPAN vol.1 $ 9.50
6. BIRDS of JAPAN $10.00
7. MAMMALS of JAPAN $10.00
8. SEASHORE ANIMALS of JAPAN $10.00
9. GARDEN FLOWERS vol.1 $ 8.50
10. GARDEN FLOWERS vol.2 $ 8.50
11. ROSES and ORCHIDS $10.00
12. ALPINE FLORA of JAPAN vol.1 $ 9.50
13. ROCKS $ 9.50
14. ECONOMIC MINERALS $10.50
15. HERBACEOUS PLANTS of JAPAN vol.1 $11.00
16. HERBACEOUS PLANTS of JAPAN vol.2 $12.50
17. HERBACEOUS PLANTS of JAPAN vol.3 $13.50
18. SEAWEEDS of JAPAN $10.00
19. TREES and SHRUBS of JAPAN $11.00
20. EXOTIC AQUARIUM FISHES vol.1 $10.00
21. MOTHS of JAPAN vol.1 $11.00
22. MOTHS of JAPAN vol.2 $11.00
23. FUNGI of JAPAN vol.1 $10.00
24. PTERIDOPHYTA of JAPAN $10.50
25. SHELLS of JAPAN vol.2 $10.50
26. FISHES of JAPAN vol.2 $ 9.50
27. EXOTIC AQUARIUM FISHES vol.2 $10.00
28. ALPINE FLORA of JAPAN vol.2 $ 9.00
29. FRUITS $ 9.50
30. REPTILES and AMPHIBI- ANS of JAPAN $ 9.50
31. ECONOMIC MINERALS vol.2 $11.00
32. FRESHWATER FISHES of JAPAN $10.50
33. GARDEN PLANTS of the WORLD vol.1 $ 9.50
34. GARDEN PLANTS of the WORLD vol.2 $ 9.50
35. GARDEN PLANTS of the WORLD vol.3 $ 9.50
36. GARDEN PLANTS of the WORLD vol.4 $10.50
37. GARDEN PLANTS of the WORLD vol.5 $11.00
38. THE FRESHWATER PLANKTON OF JAPAN $10.50
39. MEDICINAL PLANTS of JAPAN $10.00

40. VEGETABLE CROPS of JAPAN $ 8.50
41. FARM ANIMALS of JAPAN $ 9.00
42. FUNGI of JAPAN vol.2 $10.50
43. SHELLS of the WORLD vol.1 $ 8.50
44. SHELLS of the WORLD vol.2 $10.00
45. THE MARINE PLANKTON of JAPAN $11.00
46. EARLY STAGES of JAPANESE MOTHS vol.1 $10.00
47. EARLY STAGES of JAPANESE MOTHS vol.2 $ 10.50
48. FOSSILS $12.50
49. HERBACEOUS PLANTS of JAPAN vol.4 (coming issue)
50. HERBACEOUS PLANTS of JAPAN vol.5 (coming issue)

Second Issues (Book Size 7" x 10")

1. BUTTERFLIES of FORMOSA $15.50
2. EARLY STAGES of JAPANESE BUTTERFLIES vol.1 $12.50
3. EARLY STAGES of JAPANESE BUTTERFLIES vol.2 $12.50
4. SPIDERS of JAPAN $13.50
5. THE PLANKTON of JAPANESE COASTAL WATERS $10.00
6. BIRDS' LIFE in JAPAN vol.1 $12.50
7. BIRDS' LIFE in JAPAN vol.2 $12.50
8. CAGE BIRDS $12.50
9. WORLD FOLK COSTUMES $13.00
10. ATLAS of WOOD $15.00
11. PLANTS of JAPAN in their Environment $12.50
12. SPRING FLORA of SIKKIM HIMALAYA $15.50

Third Issues (Book Size 6" x 8")

1. INSECTS' LIFE in JAPAN vol.1 $12.50
2. INSECTS' LIFE in JAPAN vol.2 $12.50